I0531249

THE WISE MAN SAY

The Wise Man Say

J. A. FAULKERSON

ALSO BY J. A. FAULKERSON

Adinkrahene: Fear of a Black Planet
(Novel)

Real Men Raise CHAMPIONS: Unleashing Your Inner Coach
(Inspirational)

Young Achiever Playbook: Planning To Achieve
(Inspirational)

The Thug Whisperer
(Short Story)

Significant Brother
(Unproduced Screenplay)

A Different Kind of Prejudice
(Unproduced Screenplay)

Scan QR Code Below
To Access Purchase Links

THE WISE MAN SAY
Selected Poems

by
J. A. Faulkerson

Copyright © 2023 by Jeffery A. Faulkerson
All rights reserved.

This is a work of fiction. Names, characters, places, and incidents either are
the product of the author's imagination or are used fictitiously. Any resem-
blance to actual persons, living and dead, events, or locales is entirely coinci-
dental.

ISBN: 979-8-9910333-3-6

First Printing

No part of this publication may be reproduced, stored in or introduced into a
retrieval system, or transmitted, in any form, or by any means (electronic,
mechanical, photocopying, recording, or otherwise), without the prior writ-
ten consent of the copyright owner.

Published by
J. A. Faulkerson Books
Entertain. Educate. Enlighten.
www.jafaulkerson.wordpress.com

For
Regina & Caleb

Together, we rise.

CONTENTS

1. The Seed

2. Waxing Poetic

3. The Wise Man Say

4. Protect Me

5. Agent of Change

6. Spaceship Earth

7. When Being Black Was Cool

8. A Slave to Your Brokenness

9. Busboy To Poet

10. Reflections of That Moment

11. Black Wall Street Pervades

12. The Friend at the Door

13. Black Insurrection

14. Age of Enlightenment

15. Four Pillars of Prosperity

16. The Big Show

17. Sweat

18. My Pretty, Little, Black Girl

19. No Haven for Lower-Case Gods

20. BONUS CONTENT: Junior Achievement

THE SEED

This small, ebony seed
Tells my story, says
"Where do I go from here?"
It in my hand,
I on its exterior,
Locked together by
A bond of commonality.

Murky innards of
A world gone mad,
Soil hardening daily,
Extracting the gift of life
From our beings,
Pushing us
Lower,
Lower,
Lower,
Until darkness becomes
A home.

From the depths of the world
We dream.
Soft, moist soil, with the
Sun shining brightly
Among the heavens.
Employment.
Marriage.
Success.
Reality revealing soil
Devoid of nutrients.

Dream deferred.

We desire love,
Rain that invigorates,
Rejuvenates,
And lets one know
Someone cares.

WAXING POETIC

I feel nothing, but I know something is there, The Urge that has been with me since birth, wanting to be seen, to be heard.

Thoughts.

Emotions.

Theories.

Wanting to be expressed, to receive their proper due.

Part of me wants to push The Urge down, deep.

Keep it buried.

Hidden.

The full expression of The Urge could bring about shame, ridicule from others.

But then I remind myself that I am a
Storyteller, a Writer, and maybe a Poet.

But I have my doubts, about my ability to turn a phrase like Wright, Butler, Hughes, Neale-Hurston.

Of course, that's not the point, is it?

To be like Wright, Butler, Hughes, Neale-Hurston.

I must find my own authentic voice, allow it to be heard in the light of day.

Wow!

Did you feel that?

It's out.

The Urge.

To wax poetic.

But once again I hearken back to my motivation, my reason for wanting my voice to be heard, my words to be seen.

Am I expressing self so they can find something resonant in my words?

That's the name of the game, isn't it?

Creative expression.

Hoping that what comes out of you is more food for thought than nonsensical jibberish.

Never been a hack.

If anything, I want people to read my words,
And after reading them, feel more hopeful, more carefree.

How am I doing, y'all?

Y'all feeling more hopeful, more carefree?

THE WISE MAN SAY

Move forward then upward,
That's what the Wise Man say
He said do this daily
And you won't lose your way
But that's just what you did
In the Spring of eighty-eight
For you found yourself carrying
A tremendous weight

Dreams of Olympic glory,
Adoring fans calling your name
But your ailing body
Disqualified you from the game
You had to find something different,
Something new
You had to behave differently
To say that you grew.

But grew you did
You had no choice.
First in your family
To heed the Wise Man's voice.
His voice was loud,
His voice was clear
You felt his presence,
Drew the invisible him near

Clouds of doubt, uncertainty
And regret hovered overhead
Sinking feelings that could only
Be described as impending dread.

You know why this feeling
Inhabits your soul
Anxiety, depression,
Taking a toll

Roll, Daddy, roll
Like never before
Step into a future
That is bright, not a bore
Forward then upward
The Wise Man say
To keep this train a moving
You have to bow your head, pray

Pray for blessings
From the man seated on high
When you receive these blessings
You aren't supposed to cry
But when you do
Reflect on the road traversed,
Receiving the many blessings,
Never believing you were cursed

The Wise Man stands on the horizon
Marveling at all you have done
To overcome obstacles
To stand in the sun
He winks his eye
Only you can see
You bow at the waist
Thanking him, then God,
For this victory

At the apex of Achievement

You gain wisdom and sight
For you now know obstacles
Are there for knowledge, might
But you must extend your hand
To the hungry, the lost
Pull them up gently,
Remove them from the frost

PROTECT ME

Protect me from injury
Protect me from pain
Protect me from everything
As I run against the grain

Protect me from mediocrity,
Isolation and doubt
Protect me from anything
That causes me to curse, shout

Protect me when I'm weak,
Fighting to be strong
Protect me when it's obvious
I'm in the wrong

Protect me as I endure
Life's trials and tribulations
Protect me when I
Have newfound revelations

Protect me as I grab
The bull by the horn
Protect me when I'm rejected,
Another way of suffering scorn

Protect me as my body is
Buffeted by the storms of life
Protect me when being mad, stubborn,
Prevents me from being held by my wife.

Protect me when I dishonor

My family, my God
Protect me as I seek their forgiveness,
Admitting that my actions were odd

AGENT OF CHANGE

During the Winter
Of your discontent
You crave the warm embrace of Spring,
Knowing it will fade away to
The scintillating heat
Of Summer.
But you need not worry.
No!
Because you know that every hot Summer
Gives way to the
Coolness of Autumn.

But as the seasons change,
So do you.
You think.
You feel.
You do.
You ask yourself,
"Who am I?"
"What is my purpose
In life?"
When you ask these questions,
You expect a response,
But none is given.

Poverty often denies you access
To prosperity.
Each time, she asks,
"Can you spare a dime?"
You look into her blood-shot eyes,
And your shared silence becomes

A clarion call.

You hear voices,
Those of the great African kings
Speaking to you.
You hear the rhythmic beat of drums,
Encouraging you to dance.
This is your moment, your
Chance to shine.
But do you change or
Do you remain the same?

Heroes have come.
Heroes have gone.
But now you are being asked to be something more.
No one is asking you to change the world.
Change a life,
And bear witness to the
Rippling effects
Of your sacrifice.

SPACESHIP EARTH

Building bridges that link the present to the past is supposed to be Black folk business. But I dare say we Black folk aren't paying attention. You see, when they talk about AP Black History not being relevant enough, what they're really saying is Black folk don't matter. We matter. This country, this America, was built on Black folks' backs.

Our LEGACY is that enslaved Black Africans made a way out of no way, turned lemons into lemonade. We have all heard about Martin and his dream, about Malcolm's admonition to demand equal justice and protections by any means necessary. But did you hear about Nat Turner, the fearlessness he displayed to break free of his chains? Did you hear about him cutting the Conquering Oppressor's throat when he refused to grant him equal rights, equal protections? This descendant of Black African kings and queens was no longer playing games. He had shed too much blood and sweat, cried too many tears. Being granted privileges, rights, were no longer options, they were imperatives.

The privileges that we Black folk have today were made possible by the ACTIVISM of Sojourner Truth, Frederick Douglass, Ida B. Wells and Marcus Garvey, to name only a few. But even today, we have to remind the people who aren't Black that "Black lives matter!" Our contemporary voices are being drowned out by the Conquering Oppressor and his minions in their crusade to make America great again.

We know what they really want.

We weren't born yesterday.

Their intent is to make America White again.

This cloud, this threat, demands a response, one that continues to be nonviolent, but pierces the hearts, the minds, the souls, of anyone who believes in the power of diversity, equity and inclusion, love, justice and peace.

You see, appealing to heart, mind and soul is what will allow us to build the Beloved Community, which is synonymous with creating a more perfect union. We must learn to co-exist or cease to exist.

In this Beloved Community, this More Perfect Union, we can't afford to be more powerful than them, more superior to them. We must be willing to learn from them, them from us.

They must be willing to hear our grievances, and as they listen to what we have to say, we must also listen for the sincerity in their voices as they apologize for their crimes against humanity – committed today and back in the day.

"Black Power" was once our rallying cry, but "Power to the People," all the people, is what makes communities possible, allows them to thrive.

Our focus is always on skin color, as if we can't see that all humans have ten fingers, ten toes. I have no problem with Black solidarity – it's needed now more than ever because Black folks' liberties are under siege.

Wouldn't it be great if we could place more emphasis on KINSHIP, our connection to each other, on this birth-embarked flight aboard Spaceship Earth.

WHEN BEING BLACK WAS COOL

I was born in 1968.

That same year, 16 days after my birth, an assassin's bullet sent the Rev. Dr. Martin Luther King, Jr. home to be with his maker. They say he was being too vocal, that he forgot his place.

But history reveals that Black folk are the descendants of African kings and queens.

The desire to be excellent is in our DNA.

I remember when being Black was cool.

As a child of the late 60s, 70s and 80s, I often find myself reflecting on childhood memories of my mother's boyfriend throwing LPs on the turn table.

There was Stevie Wonder.

There was Aretha Franklin.
There was Marvin Gaye.

And let's not forget Midnight Star, their chant of "Operator. This is an emergency."

But it wasn't just the music that moved me.

Representations of our smiling, Black faces could also be seen in TV, film.

There was Good Times, The Jeffersons and What's Happening on the small screen, and Shaft, Foxy Brown and Super Fly on the big.

And I couldn't get enough of Red Foxx's Fred Sanford, especially when he placed his hand on his chest and told his beloved Elizabeth that he was coming to be with her in eternity.

These were firsts for me, of seeing Black men, Black women, marching to the beats of their own drums, totally free from the influence of White prejudice, White discrimination, White racism.
I remember when being Black was cool.

But then Dr. Bill Cosby vowed to do more to raise Black America's profile. He introduced America to his animated characters Fat Albert and the Cosby Kids, part of CBS's Saturday morning cartoon lineup.

Fat Albert didn't seem like the best representation of Blackness – he was morbidly obese – but a deeper dive reveals that Dr. Cosby created a character who was undeniably guided by a moral compass.

Fat Albert had a deep, abiding love for his friends, the Cosby Kids, and he was wired by his creator to bend over backwards to aid others in their time of need.

I remember when being Black was cool.

I will never discount the positive impact Dr. Cosby's creations had on my sense of self-worth, my ability to build a platform for success. You see, in the 80s, being Black was cool, so cool, because of Cosby-produced shows like The Cosby Show and A Different World.

The first depicted two, Black professional parents responsibly raising four, sometimes trifling, kids.

The second was a tip of the hat to Historically Black Colleges and Universities, which also inspired a racially diverse generation of high school students to pursue higher education.

I remember when being Black was cool.

Sadly, we find ourselves under attack by the Red Hats.

They saw, and continue to see, the association between being Black and being cool.

Thank the Jacksons (with Michael's bark being the loudest), Prince, Aretha Franklin, Run DMC, Patti Labelle and MC Hammer for that.

The Red Hats saw their White children developing an appreciation, respect, for Black history, Black culture. They also saw that their White children didn't want to misconstrue Black history, co-opt Black culture; they wanted to lift up Black history, lift up Black culture.

Elected Red Hat-wearing leaders now craft and institute laws that condition Blacks and other persons of color to speak less about White America's ongoing crimes and microaggressions against them.

Consequently, the conditioned silence of these same Blacks and other persons of color gives contemporary White Americans license to continue committing crimes and microaggressions against them.

I long for days when being Black becomes cool again.

A SLAVE TO YOUR BROKENNESS

I do miss you, but let's be honest with each other. I really didn't know you.

I know you would agree.

But why didn't I know you, you me?

I am flesh of your flesh, bone of your bone, but it's as if we were from two different nations, two different worlds.

I know you experienced hardship, pain, at a very early age. Always being compared to your siblings, challenged to be as good or greater than them. But you couldn't keep up. When you were alive, you led what some would consider a mediocre existence.

I get it.

But even before the 14-year-old thug in me ended your life that fateful night in nineteen eighty-two, I had been cursing you for years for deliberately going out of your way to transfer a portion of your brokenness to me.

I tried to draw close to you when I was much younger. When I did, I wanted to ask why you left my mother when I was four to fend for herself, to raise me all by herself.

My mother weathered the storm. She courageously punched her way through her fear, frustration and self-doubt, leaning on the seven siblings who knew blood is thicker than water.

They didn't browbeat my mother into pulling herself up by her bootstraps like some others do. If anything, they supported her both emotionally and financially.

And her mother, my maternal grandmother, didn't allow her, us, to pity the foolishness of it all. She made the Thanksgiving and Christmas holidays special, preparing feasts that included her signature homemade yeast rolls.

I see a lot of my maternal grandmother in my mother - hard exterior, kind heart.

I saw how your chest swelled when they called my name as a high school freshman.

My athletic exploits impressed you, didn't they?

Not going to lie, my chest swelled as well, when I caught those glimpses of pride etched on your dark, smiling face.

But where was the love, where were the words, "I love you," when I, again, drew close to you.

Was it all about you, the utterance of your last name after the utterance of my first?

I am broken, caged now like a feral animal.

I have you to blame for that.

You see, when you failed to tell me that you loved me, others, specifically the ones on my mother's side, provided the loving companionship I needed to know that I am loved. They didn't have to tell me; they showed me each time they drew close to me.

I miss that.

They drawing close to me.

I don't hate you for breaking me. The greatest gift you gave me was the sight of you suppressing your brokenness to give your new family the love and support you never gave me.

You seemed happy.

You seemed content.

And, again, I got it.

That apology you owed me, the one that had always been on the tip of your tongue, was better said than not.

Now, as I sit here turning stale within these cinderblock walls, my hatred for you grows.

The nerve!

Putting your hands on my mother.

Getting mad because she called you a deadbeat to your face.

The truth hurt, didn't it?

Of course, that truth didn't stop you from beating her into a bloody pulp, did it?

I just hope in your death, you understand why the 14-year-old thug in me had to stand up to you for her, to end you.

I have been a slave to your brokenness for far too long.

Now, I am a forever slave, not to you but to your brokenness, for that is all that remains.

All I ever needed was the gift of your apology, and words, assurances really, that you even loved me at all.

BUSBOY TO POET

I walked through the door
Expecting a crowd to be there
But the chairs were empty,
The tables, bare
I came here seeking
Open Mic, give me props
My moment of validation,
Pulling up all stops

I smiled at the lady
Seated to my right
Nodded at the gentleman
Holding her hand tight
He need not worry
I'm a married man
Make the most of this time,
More poetry written, master plan

The great Langston Hughes
Bussed tables, you hear?
The apprenticeship he needed,
To shift to another gear
So, I gripped my pen tightly,
With paper spread out
Was time to write poetry,
The kind people talk about

Not here stressing
About fortune and fame
Education, enlightenment,
Cause to reframe

The way one thinks about
Society's woes
Solving complex problems,
Reaping the positivity we sow

We poets wax poetic
On lives once led
Weaving tales of wonder,
Realities free of dread
I endeavor to write poetry
That injects hope and aspiration
But what I hope to do
Is an act of desperation

You see, I've been a struggling artist
For way too long
Published books independently,
Probably did it wrong
But this paper before me
Is a way to correct
The stroke of my pen,
Making readers connect

These readers want to see
Our triumphs and our losses
Our words becoming masterpieces
Reminiscent of a shining Colossus
Busboy to Poet
You are my inspiration
Thank you for your poetry
To be a better creation

REFLECTIONS OF THAT MOMENT

Today, I awoke to reflections of that moment.

The day we met in the bookstore, on the UT campus, way back in nineteen eighty-eight.

Your friend, your teammate, introduced us. After taking stock of this package, the parts of me that you could see, you glanced down at my shoes.

Black Reeboks.

The walkers.

They were clean, so I guess they reflected kindly on me.

We talked for hours on end after that, about politics, sports, our hopes, our aspirations.

During our time together, we have created many memories, many joyful moments to reflect on.

You, dressed in white, being escorted to the altar by your uncle.

The two of us sipping coconut juice through a straw on the island of Maui.

Our adult son and us traveling to Europe for the first time, toasting with glasses of champagne atop Paris' Eifel Tower.

I'm a country boy, raised by a single parent in Upper East Tennessee. But being with you hasn't just made my day, it has had a transformative effect on my life.

Yes, there are times when these reflections become a little fuzzy. That's what happens after more than thirty years of marriage. The ebbs, the flows, of life cause us to drift apart, repeatedly. But we made commitments to each other, bold proclamations that the other would always be there.

I attribute these drifts to my selfish ambition, unwise attempts to focus on me rather than us.

We're supposed to reflect kindly on those moments spent together. For what is success, achievement, when there's no one by your side to share it with?

Did I achieve my hopes, my dreams, the things that I talked about during our courtship?

Am I harboring bitterness, resentment, blaming you for my failing to get where I said I would be?

What we have accomplished together means more than what we could, or can, accomplish apart.

Our consummation created life, a new being, our son.

I told myself then, as I watched his newborn-self push past your vaginal walls, that he alone would be our crowning achievement. Thus, it is no longer about me getting to where I want to be. It's about him becoming all that he is meant to be.

Our son is in college now, discovering himself, trying to become independently fearless and empowered.

We did our part, communicated to him the importance of being a Great Nurturer, a Great Learner, a Great Worker, and a Great Leader. In time, we will learn if these communications were heeded, or fell on deaf ears.

This, my Queen, is what I think about when I reflect on that moment.

BLACK WALL STREET PERVADES

Nikole Hannah-Jones
Has a mighty bark
She spearheads a project
To give us Black people a spark
What she does for us
Is a selfless act
To adjoin our history to America's
In hopes of cultivating a pact

Unenlightened Whites reject her
In their quest to be right
To shake free of accountability,
Crimes committed out of spite
They're now on a quest
To recast their lot as heroes
Ignore our many grievances,
Relegate us to ground zeroes

We know that they want
To be freed from their guilt
But they persist in casting lies, dispersions,
Hoping we will wilt
But the more they call Black history
CRT
The more we chant, "Black Lives Matter!"
Not just to acquire a victory

America owes a debt
To the Black American race
Life as we know it,
Occupation of this Earthly space

Our stories, contributions, weren't
Meant to be suppressed
Our ties to African royalty,
Our agenda not repressed

They ban Black authors,
The power of their pens
All to erase all knowledge
Of their reprehensible sins
Their contemporaries say
They never played a part
In the oppression that Blacks suffered
After leaving the slave mart

Ibram X. Kendi
Probably said it best
Be an anti-racist
Remain different from the rest
1619 was the year,
Our African ancestors in chains
But we, their contemporaries,
Aren't supposed to echo their pain

In 1776,
Enslaved Africans not part of the plan
They weren't even considered
1/5 of a man
But now that they see us
In all our different shades
Let's strive to be excellent,
Black Wall Street pervades

THE FRIEND AT THE DOOR

Child Protective Services
Responds to abuse and neglect
The people that work there,
Heroes known to reflect
On lives filled with hardship,
Misery and pain
So, standing in the gap for children
Isn't a drain

Sure, its people have moments
Where their energy is spent
But they wake up each morning,
Admonishing abusers to repent
For hitting, slapping,
Taking indecent liberties
Robbing children of their innocence,
Bright destinies

When they're standing at your door,
It's not to take your children away
Greeting caring, supportive parents
Is what makes their day
My message to parents,
Have love in your heart
For your children deserve
To get off to a fresh start

Children don't need childhoods
They'd rather forget
Parents shouldn't make mistakes
That sow deep-seated regret

Being a parent,
The highest of calls
CPS workers are there
To soften their falls

Restorative justice
When these parental falls are too great
Their children now carrying
A tremendous weight
They thought their parents loved them,
Intentionally raising them to be strong
Never dawned on these children
That they could be completely wrong

So, when you see a CPS worker
Standing at your door
Invite her in,
This Saint to the core
I promise she won't cause you
To become downcast, blue
She's a friend that has agape love
For your children and you

BLACK INSURRECTION

We all saw what happened
On 1-6-21
The Red Hats stormed the Capitol
Believing their candidate had won
They came to DC
To stop the steal
But the desecration of memorials,
Couldn't believe it was real

I immediately started wondering
If this had happened in '95
When Black people came to Washington
To keep Dr. King's dream alive
He saw a nation, Black and White
Walking hand in hand
Marching to the rhythms
Of a different band

There definitely would have been bloodshed,
This I know
White people, pins and needles,
Anticipating our violent blow
But that blow never came
Probably never will
We're a peaceful, loving people
Envied for our perseverance, skill

The Black Insurrection
Is already in motion
Gathering Place and HQ DC,
Mobilizing for a promotion

Marches and sit-ins,
They're still needed today
But now that the chess game is level,
We respond in nonviolent ways

Go to college,
Graduate with a degree
Secure gainful employment,
Become a different pedigree
Social entrepreneurship
Is the thing Black people must master
Anything less,
Inviting disaster

Nothing   wrong   with   owning   businesses

That make a profit
But for us, the Black Diaspora,
More of us must rise above it
Each one, teach one,
We all getting paid
Equal   justice,   protec-
tion
No longer delayed

No sorrow for the Red Hats,
Hate and division they wrought
They ignore our real grievances
Their friendship we sought
They ban our books
Label our history CRT
But losers they all are
Citizens united, bright destiny

AGE OF ENLIGHTENMENT

Remember that conversation we had, the one about the Age of Enlightenment.

I told you it was a time, during the 17th and 18th centuries, when Western Europeans deliberated over the value of human happiness, our collective pursuit of knowledge.

Sadly, those days have long passed.

We contemporary Americans find ourselves hating more, loving less. Moreover, we encase ourselves, our groups really, into silos. But all this isolation does is keep the darker skinned peoples in their place while the descendants of the Conquering Oppressor partake freely of their unmerited privilege.

You see, the wind blows kindly on the descendants of the Conquering Oppressor. Their ancestors viewed the inhabitants of inhabited lands as savages for the way they worshipped, for just living simply with nature. To them, an intervention was necessary. Use Christianity to save indigenous souls.

Trifling then and even more so now, as the descendants of the Conquering Oppressor feign supremacy.

Pillaging vibrant, indigenous communities and ending innocent, indigenous lives in the name of an unseen but all-knowing God.

Suppressing discussion about the misdeeds that allowed them to attain control over indigenous minds, bodies, souls.

Blasphemy!

Instead of celebrating the cultural distinctiveness of the indigenous, the Conquering Oppressor schemed, ultimately co-opting many of the traditions and customs that were central to the way the indigenous communed.

We all deserve to be happy, my siblings in the struggle. And the acquisition and exchange of knowledge should be an integral part of existing. Knowing is the common denominator that adds positive dividends to the numerator, the numerous.

But how do we respond to alternative facts – lies misrepresentations, that sow confusion, chaos and conflict?

Do we allow these alternative facts to stand?

No.

Proponents of collective happiness must more forcefully counter alternative facts with absolute truths.

Truth be told, we prove ourselves enlightened when we replace hatred with love.

Truth be told, we prove ourselves enlightened when we welcome the descendants of the Conquering Oppressor as they emerge from their cocoons of retrospection to become compassionate neighbors.

Truth be told, we prove ourselves enlightened when we are guided by a shared happiness that allows us to become the righteous change we want to see in the world.

That last part is worth repeating. The part about becoming the righteous change we want to see in the world.

The Conquering Oppressor considered his soul-saving campaign righteous. We know now his actions were foul, unholy and unrighteous.

He did things his way, led by some fabricated belief that he alone was ordained to subdue the world and its savages.

But the indigenous weren't savages. They are like him, humans all, and they knew, without being told, that the Creator's judgement was imminent.

If the descendants of the Conquering Oppressor don't wake up, I dare say the Creator will not judge them kindly, for they alone are the harborers of confusion, chaos and conflict.

Their capacity to give has always been there, for they worship a God who is both loving and merciful. But this worship is a tainted kind of worship when these descendants walk around thinking they're lower-case gods.

Stop?

The higher case God bids all of us to bow before his throne of mercy and grace. To do his will.

And what is his will?

Treat others the way you want to be treated.

Give and watch him give it back to you.

Cherish wisdom, stability and peace.

Be happy.

Be knowledgeable.

Achieve enlightenment.

Together.

FOUR PILLARS OF PROSPERITY

Nurture healthy relationships
With your elders, your wife
Cherish the moments,
Live a morally righteous life
Raise children who respect themselves,
The young and the old
Hearts filled with courage,
Champions we parents mold

Learn from other people,
The books that you read
The books that they ban
Are the ones that you need
And don't forget about
The things and the places
Scale the hills to Alhambra,
Develop compassion for different races

Work to develop skills
That allow you to be more
Embrace your apprenticeship,
Strengthen your core
The tycoons of old
Showed us the way
Workers becoming owners,
A debt to them we pay

Lead with integrity,
Extend kindness and love
Under-achieving neighbors near us
Who just need a shove

Always stand
with the hungry and the lost
Remember where you came from,
All that achievement cost

These Four Pillars of Prosperity,
Independently fearless, empowered
Young Achiever becomes older,
Never again a coward
But when the pace of your ascension
Should ever slow down
Just remember your ancestors were royalty,
On your head sits a crown

THE BIG SHOW

I held you in my arms,
Said, "What could be better than this?"
A kiss on the lips
A cool Winter bliss?
No! The sight of you
The feather in my cap
For you first came to me
When I was taking a nap

When my eyes were closed
I dreamed of you
Turning two into three
To faraway lands we flew
Yes, I have this dream
Of becoming a famous writer
But having you in my present
Has made my future much brighter

These days, I don't think much
About literary success
You want to know why?
Take a guess
You, I proclaim boldly
For this much I know
All that I am, all that I want to be
Is for you, the Big Show

Those stories you tell me
In your squeaky voice
Are meant to be on paper,
So, make the choice

Stop hoarding your words,
Like they're better in than out
You are the writer
They should be talking about

If you remember one thing,
Remember this
You are my crowning achievement,
Hit or miss
You have shown that you have
The capacity to be great
Bear down, my son,
Reach a different state

Your writing will be reflective
Of your goals, your passions
Characters in situations
Clothed in ancient fashions
I know you like to write about
Soldiers, war
Simple stories worth telling,
Never knowing what's in store.

So, I leave you now
About to step off this stage
But before I go
I bid you to engage
Your audience is out there
So, I need you to listen
The Big Show has arrived
On you I christen

SWEAT

Why do you come here?

Why do you feel the need to sweat?

Every other day, you drag yourself to this place, this gym, working out your legs on Tuesdays and Saturdays, your chest, arms and abs on Thursdays and Sundays. You know you're building muscle, you may even be losing weight.

But why?

Why do you do it?

I see what you see.

There are a lot of pretty women up in this joint.

Some PHAT - Pretty, Hot and Tempting.

Others just fat, or a little pudgy – like the middle-aged you.

That one has a pretty face.

That one has a shapely figure.

Damn! That dude has arms for legs.

Is that why you come here, to this communal space?

To admire the pretty and shapely women?

The dudes with arms for legs?

Not believing that.

Your wife would put them all to shame.

I seen her.

She pretty.

She shapely.
She downright sexy.

But thank God she doesn't have arms for legs.

Look who just showed up at the front desk.

Your adult son.

He almost 21, right?

Still trying to figure things out, huh?

Boy entering his second year of college.

Great potential that boy has. He a hard worker – smart as all get-all – and he has never been one to bite the hand that feeds him.

Watch out, now. One day he gonna show up at your crib with a facsimile of one of these pretty, shapely females that don't have arms for legs. They gonna go steady for a while, and possibly get engaged and then married to expand your family even more.

So, that's it.

I see what you doing, why you spend all of this time sweating in the midst of strangers.

You trying to add longevity to your life.

What's this?

Look who just stepped onto the gym floor.

Your wife.

She already sweating from her three-mile outdoor run.

Damn, Slim. Y'all need to save all that kissing for the bedroom.

Almost goes without saying that you want to have a more adventurous life with your wife. Having an empty nest does have its advantages.

But you also want to be around to welcome your daughter-in-law to the family, greet each of your grandchildren moments after they exit your daughter-in-law's womb.

Sweat on, my brother.

Sweat on.

MY PRETTY, LITTLE BLACK GIRL

A pretty, little, black girl
In the grocery store
She wasn't much older
Than the age of four
Her skin was jet black,
Her eyes, green
Her hair was curly,
Afro Sheen

Heavy-set, black lady
Standing by her side
Mean look on her face,
Remarks that were snide
She smacked the girl once
On the top of her hand
She said buying her a toy
Wasn't part of the plan

She looked up at me,
Standing behind her in line
I saw a tear on her cheek,
If only she were mine
I would buy her that toy,
Put a smile on her face
Spoil her rotten,
Extend her mercy, grace

Fond memories I have
About the son that I'm raising
Awards and honors received,
Other people praising

Pregnancy that preceded him,
What a terrible loss
Seeing my pretty, little, black girl
Wearing lip gloss

The heavy-set, black lady turned
Glared back at me
The lines in her face spoke volumes,
Please let us be
But I picked up the toy
Snatched from the little girl's hand
Placed it on the belt,
Shoulder shrug, silent command

The pretty, little, black girl wiped
The tears from her face
She stood a little taller,
Please pick up the pace
But the heavy-set, black lady
Waved my payment away
I paused briefly,
Giving her time to get out my way

I placed the purchased toy
In the pretty, little, black girl's hand
The heavy-set, black lady relented,
Some elaborate plan?
"What do you say?" I heard the heavy-set, black lady ask
"Thank you," the pretty, little, black girl said,
Completing the task

Moments like these
Cause me to think of you
Losing you then

Makes me feel a little blue
Oh, to have seen you learning
At the knee of your mother,
Being a friend, a mentor,
To your little brother

NO HAVEN FOR LOWER CASE GODS

The Good Book says faith is the assurance of things hoped for, the promise of things not seen. But to my dismay, I'm starting to lose faith in people.

These days, people aren't guided by their faith; they're guided by their politics, or better put, they allow their politics to guide their faith. They're wrong, especially when you consider this thing we Americans are hoping for: the creation of A More Perfect Union.

No one said union creation would be easy. And it becomes even more complicated when the citizens of this union start segregating themselves based on skin color.

Haven't we been called to be Compassionate Neighbors, not Conquering Oppressors?

It was Dr. King who admonished us to not judge our neighbor by the color of his skin, but by the content of his character. What he saw was little, Black boys and little, Black girls walking hand in hand with little White boys and little, White girls, chanting, "Free at last. Free at last. Thank God Almighty, we're free at last."

But how can we be free of our tarnished past when a segment of our population knows the writing is there, on the wall, but refuses to acknowledge that it's there?

I live and breathe politics, but I also place it in its proper place, directly behind my faith, more specifically, my faith in God.

The fact that I watch Morning Joe during the day, The ReidOut at night, lets you know I lean Progressive, but what's wrong with that?

How can being Progressive be wrong when I'm allowing my faith in the Sovereign God to guide my politics, not allowing politics to guide my faith in the Sovereign God?

My faith in the Sovereign God causes me to adhere to the two greatest commandments –

...love the Lord your God with all your heart, with all your mind, with all your soul, and with all your strength,

...and love your neighbor as yourself.

This love for God and love for neighbor demands that I have reverence for my God, compassion for my neighbors.

Does that mean we elect leaders who naively believe they have all the answers to all the world's problems?

No!

Does that mean one segment of our population is beyond reproach?

No!

Does that mean other segments of our population should forever remain victims and not victors?

Again, no!

We need leaders who first and foremost kneel at the throne of the Sovereign God, respecting his right to give us, his creation, free will, the choice to accept the gift of eternal life with him, or reject it for eternal separation from him.

We need to have a candid conversation about global history so the Conquering Oppressor and his minions can stop thinking they're beyond reproach.

The consequence of one group thinking it is superior to all the others benefits no one, for it works to embitter all the other groups by not addressing their real concerns, their real grievances – their need to be equally served, protected and represented in our global mainstream culture.

We need the other segments of our population to think of themselves as victors, individuals not needing the validation, the endorsement, of the Conquering Oppressor.

We are children of a transformative God, and the significance of this paternity should cause us to demand full humility, full confession and full repentance from the Conquering Oppressor and his minions so all of God's children can finally get down to living independently fearless and empowered lives together.

When you find yourself kneeling at the throne of the Sovereign God, you understand that life is eternal, not temporal.

Again, I am reminded that everything done under the Sun is meaningless. That's why I choose to be an Independent, albeit one who leans Progressive.

Conservatism has us holding onto traditional, outdated values. It bids its adherents to not rock the boat, to not make waves. But I'm here to tell you that the boat needs to be rocked, waves need to be made.

While progress and technological advances are being made, we Americans still find ourselves jockeying for privilege as racialized individuals and groups.

But humanity wasn't created to be confined to these racialized prisons.

We were created to reflect the divine image of the Sovereign God.

Therefore, what good is jockeying for privilege when privilege is given freely for all eternity to those who stand with and stand for the Sovereign God?

Republican Conservative Ronald Reagan won his first presidential election largely from the support he received from Jerry Falwell's Moral Majority. These Christian Conservatives endeavored to find a counterbalance to all things secular.

But we see now that they failed miserably. They only confused matters, for we now have entire Christian congregations allowing political labels to define the contours of their faith.

I wish there was some way we could communicate with our ancestors, at least the ones who have established eternal residency with the Sovereign God.

They would undoubtedly have some harsh words for us temporal beings, and even harsher ones for those temporal beings who are guilty of confusing matters.

I dare say they would let the latter group, this so-called Moral Majority, know that there is nothing moral about what they're doing.

The Moral Majority has given once-loyal Jesus Christ followers license to demonize Central American asylum seekers, or migrants.

The Moral Majority has given once-loyal Jesus Christ followers license to suppress, and in some instances, erase, the histories of Blacks, the Indigenous, and other persons of color.

The Moral Majority has given once-loyal Jesus Christ followers license to ignore the deplorable behavior of a former president who...

...paid a porn star to remain silent about his extramarital affair,

...got charged and held liable for sexual assault and financial fraud,

...has been indicted for stealing and maintaining classified government documents at his Florida resort,
...bilked millions of dollars from his supporters off a lie about a free and fair election being stolen from him,

...and has been indicted for inciting an insurrection, which saw his supporters storm the U. S. Capitol Building, resulting in five senseless deaths.

More than anything, though, this Moral Majority has made it more difficult for the Body of Christ to fulfill the Great Commission.

We Christians are supposed to be about the business of making disciples of all the nations, baptizing them in the name of the Father, Son and the Holy Spirit, with the promise that he will stand with us to the very end of the age.

So, I'm tired of all this talk about Christian Nationalism.

Christian Nationalism cannot exist within the boundaries of the Sovereign God's eternal, Heavenly Kingdom.

We're Children of God, period, and we come in all sizes, shades and colors.

But I feel bad for the people who have become transplants of this man-made Christian nation, foolishly thinking their political ideology reflects their Christianity.

Power, influence and control are at the top of their minds.

That is the focus of a conqueror.

That is the focus of an oppressor.

Sadly, such a focus relegates individuals, groups even, to the role of the Conquering Oppressor, and his primary aim is to be considered a lower-case god.

However, the Sovereign God's eternal Heavenly Kingdom – his more perfect union – is no haven for lower-case gods.

Let's pray that our collective faith in the Sovereign God compels us to celebrate the Compassionate Neighbor and denounce the Conquering Oppressor.

BONUS CONTENT

Junior ACHIEVER
A Novel

By
J. A. Faulkerson, MSSW

My name is Luther Blevins, Jr., but most people just call me Junior, or LJ. And one of the first things I want you to know about me is I didn't always know I was young, gifted and black.

Didn't really make sense then, especially during the summer before my freshman year at Etiwanda Intermediate School. That was the summer when the lives of everyone in my family took a turn for the worse.

You see, my mother Serenity Rawlings was seeing this dude – Pete Burnett – who worked as a baggage handler at the Ontario/San Bernardino Airport. Pete seemed like a cool dude, someone who treated us like we were his own children during his long-term relationship with our mother. He was also the kind of man who made Moma feel like the queen that she is.

My older sister Alana was about to enter her senior year at EIS, and, at the time, I was excited about the prospect of matriculating from the eighth grade to the ninth so I could see more of her.

Alana had lofty dreams, y'all. Standing five feet, seven inches tall, with a 40-inch vertical, she was considered one of the top shooting guards in the country. She was receiving offers to play basketball at schools like Tennessee, Stanford, LSU and Connecticut, to name only a few. To say she was my hero would be an understatement.

But it seemed those Hoop Dreams of hers would go up in smoke the summer of 1986. That was when Moma took Alana to the Kindred Hospital Emergency Room after Alana told her, a grimace on her caramel-brown face, that her stomach hurt. While at the hospital, the attending physician told Alana that her stomach had been hurting because she was already more than six weeks pregnant with a child.

I can only imagine the look on Alana's face upon hearing this news. That coming September, she would turn 18 years old. She

had spent that entire summer in the weight room and on the track, under Pete's guidance and instruction, getting her body tight so she could have her finest season ever.

The moment Pete set foot in our home, Alana immediately took a liking to him. I think it had more to do with their mutual

interest in basketball. They both were Chicago Bull fans, and felt that Michael Jordan would surpass Magic Johnson as the all-time greatest shooting guard. But Alana also enjoyed hearing Pete talk about his exploits as a star prep hoopster up in Manassas, Virginia, at Stonewall Jackson High School, and at Virginia Commonwealth University. During his freshman year at VCU, Pete led the Rams in scoring with 31 points per game. But after blowing out his knee in the first game of his sophomore season, he never suited up again.

Truth be told, when I first heard about Alana's pregnancy, I wasn't all that surprised. After she started dating Tony Napier, DB's standout tailback, my younger brother Damian and I would be upstairs in our bedroom listening as Moma explained to Alana that if she planned on having sex with Tony, she needed to make him wrap his shit up when they did it, largely because Moma had only just recently taken Alana to the doctor to get on the pill.

"Better to be safe than sorry," Moma would say. "Y'all don't need no babies right now. Too much to lose. Too much to look forward to."

After school, we knew Moma and Pete would be at work, so we kids were free to walk across the street to the V. O. Dobbins

Recreation Center, The Rec, to play or remain in the house and watch cartoons for the remainder of most weekdays. What Moma didn't know is Alana and Tony had already been up in the crib doing the nasty after school long before Moma took her to the doctor to get on the pill. And that's why I avoided sitting on the left side of the sofa when playing Pac-Man on our Nintendo

Game System with Damian. The left side was Alana and Tony's go-to spot, the place where Tony would allow Alana to rest her bare shins and ankles atop his shoulders as he drove his exposed hips into her pelvis.

After I walked in on them - their naked bodies intertwined, coated with a sheen of sweat and other bodily fluids - Alana would always plead with me not to tell Moma.

But it's not what Alana told me not to tell Moma. It's what Damian said he saw Pete doing to Alana that unsettled me.

Damian swore on Moma's grave that he had seen Pete kissing Alana on her lips, not on her cheek, more than once. He said he would usually see Pete kissing Alana out on the back patio when they thought no one could see them. I told Damian that it was nothing, that he had it all wrong, that Pete had kissed her on the cheek not on her lips. I added that Pete was just trying to make Alana feel special, like she was his daughter. But Damian, who was four years younger than me at the time, and in the fifth grade, told me it just wasn't the kiss that concerned him, it was the way Alana looked at Pete, like she was in love with him.

Fortunately for Alana, she worked with Moma to get an abortion. And, after making a full recovery during that summer before her senior year, Alana was able to resume her training for the upcoming season. But the arguments between Moma and Pete after Alana got her abortion seemed to become more frequent with each passing day.

~

"Moma! What did you do?"

It was a weeping Alana, standing in the upstairs hallway outside the bedroom that Moma had been sharing with Pete. Damian and I stumbled out of our beds, rushing into the hallway to stand behind Alana. What we saw inside the bedroom made our hearts sink.

Moma sat on the edge of her king-sized bed, her emotionless face and night gown soaked with Pete's blood. Behind her was an outstretched Pete, writhing, blood gushing from his chest and mouth, six-inch butcher knife protruding from his chest.

Alana immediately dropped to her knees, sobbing profusely into her extended hands, as Pete's once frenetic movements became less so with each passing second. Pete, the man who had been the only true father we three kids had ever known, was dying right there in front of us, and there was nothing we could do.

Alana turned to me, shouting, "Dial 911!"

I did as I was told, frantically rushing down the flight of stairs and to the wall-mounted rotary phone in the kitchen.

When the first responders - which included four paramedics and what seemed like a squadron of cops - arrived, a female cop ushered us kids outside the apartment while the paramedics tended to the carnage inside. By this time, our neighbors were lined up on the street behind yellow caution tape. After standing outside for what seemed like an eternity, we were relieved to see Moma exiting the apartment, escorted by two cops, a male on her right, female on her left. Her hands were cuffed in front of her. She peered over at us, first at Alana and then Damian and me. She mouthed the words, "I'm sorry." The cops then pushed her toward one of the squad cars parked along the curb. The female cop shielded her head as Moma dropped down onto the back seat. After shutting the back passenger door, the squad car pulled away from the curb with Moma in the back seat, its blue lights spinning, siren blaring.

"Why did Moma do that?" Damian said, peering up at Alana in hopes that she could provide an answer. But the blank stare on Alana's face let us know that she was lost in her own thoughts. Moreover, her not reaching over to pull Damian close was an indication that these same thoughts were starting to get the best of her.

I draped my arm across Damian's shoulders, even as two para-medics exited our apartment with the black body bag containing Pete's lifeless body. They threw the black body bag on the gurney that had remained on the front porch before they had entered. They then wheeled it to the gaping doors of the ambulance, the red-blue lights from the emergency response vehicles reflecting off their uniforms and the faces of the growing assembly of bystanders, us kids.

"We don't know," I finally replied. "No one knows."

But when I said that, Alana fell to her knees, bent over at the waist as her body shook vigorously from her moans, her groans. That's when a black lady with what I considered a kind face seemed to ap-pear out of nowhere.

The black lady knelt down and drew close to Alana. She whispered something into Alana's ear, something that neither Damian nor I couldn't hear. Moments later, Alana stood back up, taking time to peer over at Damian and me. As my eyes were locked onto hers, I sensed great sorrow, great regret. But it all ended when my eyes shifted to the black lady's colleague, a dark-skinned brother, stooping down to introduce himself to Damian. I deemed his actions a dis-traction, because I could clearly see the black lady leading Alana away from us over the dark-skinned brother's right shoulder.

"Alana!" I cried out, bolting toward her. But the dark-skinned brother extended his left arm to corral me, even as he held onto Damian's left arm, near the elbow. With tears glistening on my cheeks, I shifted my gaze to the dark-skinned brother.

"Where are they taking her?"

"She's going to be fine," the dark-skinned brother replied. "All of you are going to be fine."

~

Later that same night, Damian and I found ourselves at the Rancho Cucamonga Police Station on Civic Center Drive, sitting next to each other in a cramped room around an eight-foot-long table. We weren't alone. A female cop sat a few feet away from us, to the left of the doorway, occasionally peering up from the book she was reading to ask if we needed anything, water, cookies. She was only there to watch us, as the dark-skinned brother, who Damian and I learned was a Child Protective Services worker named Malcolm, had stepped out to get us something to eat.

When Mr. Malcolm returned, he bore sausage, egg and cheese biscuits and bottled orange juices that he had picked up from McDonalds. He was accompanied by a tie-wearing white dude, Detective Lynch. As Detective Lynch claimed a seat at the table across from us, Mr. Malcolm walked over to our side of the table and placed our wrapped biscuits and bottled drinks in front of us. When Mr. Malcolm saw Damian smile back at him, he gently pounded Damian's right shoulder. The female cop took the liberty to step out of the room.

"Where did they take Moma?" I asked as Mr. Malcolm joined Detective Lynch on the other side of the table. I wasn't even phased by the enticing smell emanating from the food, even though I was hungry as a mofo.

"Where's Alana?" Damian followed.

Detective Lynch and Mr. Malcolm exchanged knowing glances. I could tell they wanted to answer our pointed questions, but I also sensed that they were guarded, that they didn't want to tell us too much. But I needed them to tell us something. I needed to know what lied in store for Alana, Damian and me - for Moma even.

"Your mother is currently being detained," Detective Lynch began. "She did a bad thing, boys. And we need answers from her.
We need to know why she did what she did."

"Is she going to jail?" Damian asked.

Detective Lynch replied, "We don't know yet. Depends on what she tells us, whether she's charged with a crime or not. Just know she's okay and receiving the best treatment possible. Once she tells us why she did what she did, maybe it will all make
sense." He paused briefly, seemingly to gather his thoughts. "Did you boys see what happened?"

I could sense Damian peering over at me as I looked straight ahead, first at Mr. Malcolm then Detective Lynch.

"All we saw was Moma sitting on the bed," I replied.
"Pete was behind her, bleeding, with that big knife in him. We had gone to bed because we had school the next day."

"What were they doing before y'all went to bed?"

"They were having one of their discussion up in their room. They were talking loud, so I put my headphones on and listened to my music while I did my homework at the kitchen table. D was in the living room watching TV."

Detective Lynch shifted his attention to Damian, who had taken a bite from his biscuit and was chewing.

"Did you hear what they were talking about, Damian?"

Damian swallowed hard, seemingly prematurely, because he gagged his food back up, chewed it, and swallowed it again.

"Only heard Moma," Damian replied. "Pete really didn't say much. But I could tell Moma was crying. I could hear it in her voice. She kept asking him why he lied to her. About what, she didn't say."

"Did either of them ever come back downstairs to check on you?"

"Moma did," I interjected. "When I looked up from the book I was reading, I saw her come downstairs and sit on the couch behind Damian for a few minutes. He was sitting on the floor. She pulled him close, rested her arms on his shoulders, hugged him really. Damian had been watching Cosby, so she sat there and watched the rest of it with him. After the credits started
rolling, she came over to check on me. She then kissed me here" - I pointed to my left cheek - "before going to the kitchen. I
heard her go into the cabinet and then the fridge. I then heard her pouring juice into a glass. After she left the kitchen, she
went right back upstairs."

"Anymore arguing between her and Pete?"

"No. They had both just gotten home from work, so they were probably tired."

Mr. Malcolm asked, "Where was Alana? Was she home?"

"She was out," Damian replied, "with her boyfriend, Tony."

"Were you two awake when she got home?" Detective Lynch directed his question to me.

"I was," I replied.

Damian said, "I wasn't. I was in bed. Moma told me I could watch A Different World, but after it was over, I had to go to bed."

"Junior, what did your sister and you talk about when she got home?"

I reached for the now-cold hash brown protruding from the top of the paper wrapper and took a bite.

"I told her that they had been up in their bedroom arguing again. Told her the shit was getting old, that if Pete made her
feel so unhappy, she needed to tell him to leave."

"What did Alana have to say about that?"

"She agreed. But I could tell she really didn't want to see Pete go."

"Why? Why wouldn't she want Pete to go?"

"Pete is the reason why she's so good at basketball. During the off-season, they're always together, down at The Rec lifting weights, on the track running sprints and laps. If it wasn't for Pete, she wouldn't be getting all these scholarship offers."

"You're a pretty good athlete yourself, aren't you?" Mr. Malcolm interjected. "They're saying you could be playing on Etiwanda's varsity football team in the Fall, as a freshman. Came to one or two of your eighth games last year. You a bad dude, young buck."

I didn't know how to respond to such praise, so I opted not to say anything. I pushed the hash brown into my mouth until it was all gone.

End of
JUNIOR ACHIEVER
Chapter One

MEET THE POET

J. A. Faulkerson is a Northern Virginia-based Author, Poet and Screenwriter. His poetry pays homage to the Black leaders of the Civil Rights Movement of the 1950s and '60s, individuals he calls compassionate neighbors because they were, and continue to be, led by the unconditional love and neighborly compassion in their hearts.

J. A. also has a heart for youth, evidenced by his years of service as a TRIO Upward Bound and YMCA Youth director. Through his written and spoken words, he admonishes adolescents and young adults to balance their lives on the Four Pillars of Prosperity (i.e., Nurturing, Learning, Working and Leading).

A graduate of Dobyns-Bennett High School (Kingsport, Tennessee) and the University of Tennessee (Knoxville, Tennessee), J. A. has been happily married to his wife for over 32 years and is the proud father to his 21-year-old son.

www.ingramcontent.com/pod-product-compliance
Lightning Source LLC
Chambersburg PA
CBHW071202130626
46555CB00004B/1554